How to Make Beautiful Buttons

Beate Schmitz

Search Press

Dear reader,

The thing that I love most about buttons is their versatility: we can collect them, lose them, admire them, buy them in designer stores and even make them ourselves. I have always preferred homemade buttons; they can be eye-catching works of art and are a fantastic way to express creativity.

I have collected all my crafty button ideas for you in this book. Here you will find projects using crochet, embroidery, sewing, knotting, felting and painting. There is a variety of craft techniques so you can feel free to pick up and start wherever you like.

However, you should be warned, there's definitely something addictive about making buttons!

Best wishes,

Beate Schmitz

Contents

Each of the general techniques is explained throughout the book. In each project this symbol will indicate the specific techniue used:

Button materials

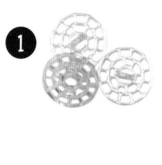

1 Plastic grid buttons: Plastic buttons with a grid on the surface are perfect for embroidering and crocheting.

2 Fabric-covered shank buttons: With a gently rounded surface that makes them ideal as a base for beaded buttons.

3 Head pins: Used to attach the shank to the chain or link.

4 Split rings: These rings are normally used for making jewellery, and can be sewn to the bottom of the button as a shank.

5 Eyes: The part of a hook-and-eye fastening that can easily be shaped to create a shank, and can be machine washed.

6 Link chain: Individual chain links are used as an extension for a button attachment.

7 Button blanks: can be crocheted over, covered or sewn onto the back of another button.

8 Backing rings: Can be used to secure any kind of button, which allows for removal before washing.

Making buttons detachable

⬤ SEWING ON BUTTONS

Many of the buttons in this book are not suitable for machine washing. But there are a few tricks for easily attaching the buttons so they can be removed for washing then reattached.

1 Backing button: Sew a backing button onto the back of your button. Secure the thread on the back of the decorative button, then attach to the backing button. Sew through the shank of the decorative button and the holes on the backing button several times, making sure you leave enough space between the two.
2 Sew a buttonhole to match the backing button in the desired place. Then the button can be buttoned in.
3 + 4 Backing rings: Here, a backing ring is used to secure your button, rather than a backing button. Insert the button shank into the appropriate place on the fabric. Attach the backing ring to the button shank – it might be an idea to use a chain link as an extension so that the button isn't too tight on the fabric.
Alternatively, instead of inserting the shank through the fabric, you could also sew a small buttonhole into the fabric. On knitted garments, it is often easy enough just to push the button shank between the stitches.

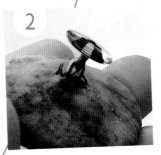

Beading & crochet

Sparkling, elegant, fabulously bright and unique – beaded buttons are wonderfully eye-catching.

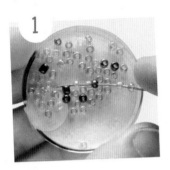

THREADING BEADS

1 Start by threading the beads onto the crochet yarn. The instructions all have a diagram indicating the bead sequence. A special bead-threading needle consisting of two wires that are joined together at the ends is ideal. The wires can be pulled apart and the yarn threaded with ease. These needles are very thin, which means that tiny rocailles (seed beads, approximately 2mm (1/16in) diameter) can also be used. As the holes in some beads will invariably be too small for the needle and thread to fit through, only thread a few beads at a time, and then push them onto the yarn.

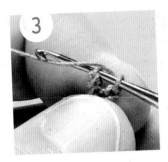

2 It is a good idea to mark the beginning of each round with a little piece of paper. Cut out some small paper squares and push a needle through the middle. The beads are crocheted in the opposite order to that on the thread. This means that the last bead to be threaded is the first one to be crocheted. In the diagrams (see page 11), the first bead to be threaded is identified by the number 1.

CROCHET ROUND TECHNIQUES

The size of the beads and buttons must match so that the beads fit tightly together.

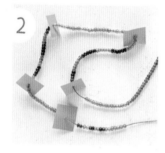

3 Once all the beads have been threaded, work five chain stitches and join in a circle with one slip stitch. Crochet tightly so that the beads are close together.

TIP: With transparent beads, the colour of the crochet yarn will shine through, changing the colour of the beads. This can be seen quite clearly in the furniture knobs on page 14.

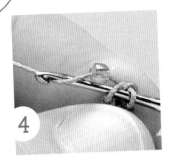

4 Continue crocheting the beads. These are single crochet stitches (UK double crochet) with beads threaded onto the yarn. Insert the hook into the back loop of the next stitch and push the first bead onto your work. Pull the yarn behind the bead and through the stitch so you have two loops on the hook. Then pull the yarn through the two loops on the hook.

5 In the first round, work one bead stitch into each chain stitch; at the end of the round the beads will form a circle. In the second round, work two and three bead stitches alternately into each stitch of the previous round = twelve stitches/beads.

⚇ CROCHETING SPIRALS

6 The instructions for each button will tell you whether to work in spirals or rounds. With spirals there is no clear transition between the rounds; simply continue working bead stitches.

If the sequence of beads makes it impossible to see the transition, use a different colour thread to mark the variation.

You need to increase the stitches in order to make a circle. To do this, work two bead stitches into each stitch on the previous row (see picture).

⚇ CROCHETING ROUNDS

7 If the pattern consists of completed rounds, the round is finished with one slip stitch into the first stitch of the round. The picture shows the free final stitch of the previous round (black arrow), the slip stitch finishing the previous round (blue arrow), the chain stitch at the transition between the rows (green arrow) and the first stitch of this round into which the slip stitch is crocheted to end the round (red arrow).

8 Then move on to the next round with one chain stitch, and crochet the first bead stitch into the first stitch of the previous round that also has the slip stitch (when increasing, also work two bead stitches at the beginning of the round).

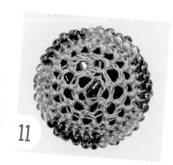

⊙ BUTTON BACK

9 Once you have worked all of the beads, secure the beginning of the thread and place the shank button on the back of the bead surface so that the stitch loops are against the outer edge of the button. Then continue working in spirals, decreasing two single crochet (UK double crochet) together.

10 Insert the hook in the first stitch, draw one loop through, insert in the second stitch, and draw through another loop so you have three loops on the hook. Draw the yarn through all three loops together.

11 Continue crocheting until the shank button is entirely covered.

Designs for beginners

Threading diagram for button A

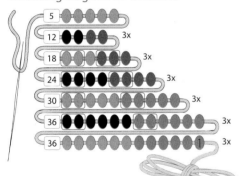

Threading diagram for button B

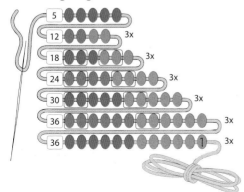

Materials (per button)

- rocailles in three different colours, 3mm (⅛in) diameter
- round shank button, approximately 27mm (1 1/16 in) diameter
- very fine crochet yarn
- crochet hook size 10–8 (1.25–1.5mm)

How it's done

Thread the beads as shown in the threading diagram. Every row in the diagram represents one round. The sequence of beads needs to be threaded three times for each round. So you start by threading six brown, six pale pink, six brown, six pink, six brown and another six pale pink beads. Thread all the other rounds accordingly.

Work five chain stitches and join with a slip stitch to make a ring. The buttons are worked in spirals. Crochet the first and second rounds. From the third round, increase at the marks. With this pattern, this means crochet two bead stitches into one stitch in the previous round when the colour changes. You will automatically increase six stitches in every round. Finish the button.

Symbols

- ⬤ = pale pink, transparent
- ⬤ = pink, opaque
- ⬤ = turquoise, transparent
- ⬤ = brown, transparent
- 18 = number of beads in this round
- ⬤⬤ = work 2 bead stitches into 1 stitch in the previous round (= increase 1)

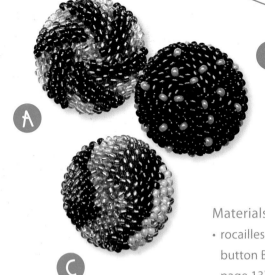

How it's done

Thread the beads as shown in the diagram. For button A, thread the recurring bead sequences in the quantity shown. The diagrams for buttons B and C show all the beads. Crochet the buttons in spirals (see page 10). The diagram for button A shows where to increase from the 3rd round on.

Materials (per button)

- rocailles, 2mm (1/16in) diameter (button A: 6 colours; button B: 2 colours; button C: 5 colours: see symbols page 13)
- round shank button, approximately 27mm (1 1/16in) diameter
- very fine crochet yarn in pale pink
- crochet hook size 11–10 (1–1.25mm)

Threading diagram for button A

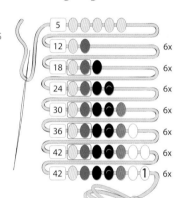

Threading diagram for button B

Threading diagram for button C

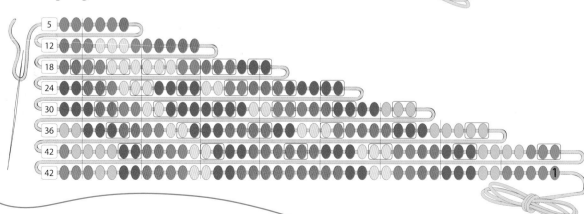

Materials (per button)

- rocailles, 2mm (1/16 in) diameter (button A: 6 colours; button B: 2 colours; button C: 5 colours: see symbols page13)
- round shank button, approximately 27mm (1 1/16 in) diameter
- very fine crochet yarn in pale pink
- crochet hook size 11–10 (1–1.25mm)

How it's done

Thread the bead sequences as shown in the diagram and in the given quantities.

Work five chain stitches and join in a ring with a slip stitch.

Crochet buttons A and B in rounds, button C in spirals (see pages 10 –11). In the second round, work two and three bead stitches alternately into each stitch of the previous round = 12 stitches. All other increases are indicated in the diagram.

Symbols

- ◐ = gold, opaque
- ○ = colourless, transparent
- ◐ = pale pink, transparent
- ◐ = pink, transparent
- ◖ = wine red, transparent
- ● = dark lilac, transparent
- ◐ = brown, transparent
- ◐ = pale turquoise, transparent
- ◐ = turquoise, transparent
- ⊗ = pale pink, opaque

42 = number of beads in this round

⬭⬭ = work 2 bead stitches into 1 stitch in the previous round (= increase 1)

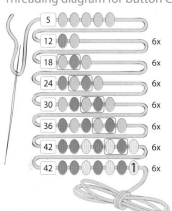

Threading diagram for button A

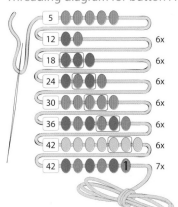

Threading diagram for button B

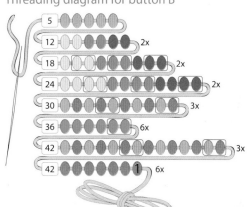

Threading diagram for button C

Furniture knobs

Crocheting them means the beads are close together and the knob is so compact that it can easily cope with the stresses of daily use.

Material

- Washers, 20 x 5mm (¾ x ¼in) (outer and inner diameter)
- book screws (sleeves approximately 10mm (³⁄₈in) long, screws to suit the thickness of the wood)
- rocailles in light blue, turquoise and dark blue, 2mm (¹⁄₁₆in) diameter
- very fine crochet yarn in white
- crochet hook size 11–10 (1–1.25mm)

TIP: Using light or dark yarn will create an entirely different look with transparent beads. Knob A is crocheted in white yarn, knob B in white on the inside and blue on the outside, and knob C all in blue yarn. The bead colours are the same on all three knobs.

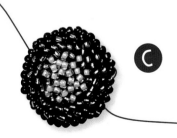

How's it done

Thread the beads as shown in the threading diagram. Work five chain stitches and join with a slip stitch to make a ring. Continue working in spirals (see pages 10–11). Push the washers onto the sleeve and place both on the back of the bead surface in place of the shank button. Continue working in spirals as for the button, decreasing two stitches each round, until the last few stitches are tight around the sleeve.

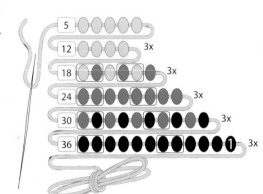

5	3x
12	3x
18	3x
24	3x
30	3x
36	1 3x

Symbols

◯ = light blue, transparent

◑ = turquoise, transparent

● = dark blue, transparent

18 = number of beads in this round

◯◑ = work 2 bead stitches into 1 stitch in the previous round (= increase 1)

Ball buttons

The smaller these are and the more there are of them, the better: a loop fastening with sparkling ball buttons is a perfect highlight on any item of clothing.

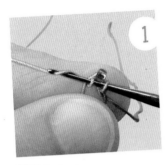

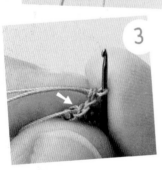

◉ CROCHETING BEADED BUTTONS

Thread the beads in accordance with the instructions.

1 + 2 Work three bead stitches into a loop of thread (see page 62). Be particularly careful with the first stitch to make sure the bead is on the outside.

3 Continue working spiral rounds in bead stitches and increase as you work. Insert the hook in the first of the three stitches (see white arrow) and work three bead stitches into this stitch. Work three bead stitches into each of the remaining two stitches = nine stitches.

4 Now carefully tighten the loop of thread.

5 To mark the end of one round and beginning of the next, pull a piece of thread in a different colour through at the beginning of the new round.

6 Bead with shank: push the rivet pin into a large bead. Trim the end of the wire to 1.5cm (½in) with the wire cutters, then fold over with some pliers and push the end of the wire into the hole.

7 Continue working as described in the instructions. Then push the bead and shank into the crochet and start to decrease. Insert the needle in the next stitch, push one bead onto the crochet work, and draw through one loop.

Insert the hook in the next stitch, slide another bead onto the work and draw a loop through so that you have three loops on your hook. Yarn around the hook and draw through all three loops on the hook.

8 Decreasing will close the stitches around the shank. The bead is worked into your crochet.

Material

- rocailles, 2mm (¹/₁₆in) diameter
- very fine crochet yarn thickness in a matching colour
- for the large ball button: Bead, 10mm (³/₈in) diameter
- for the small ball button: Bead, 8mm (⁵/₁₆in) diameter
- rivet pin
- crochet hook size 11–10 (1–1.25mm)
- pliers
- wire cutters

How it's done

Large button: thread 111 beads. Start with a loop of thread (see pages 16 and 62) with three bead stitches, and crochet nine bead stitches in the second round. In the third round, work two bead stitches into each stitch of the previous round = eighteen beads. Crochet three rounds of bead stitches without increasing. Push the shank bead (see page 16) into the crochet, and in the next round decrease two bead stitches together = nine stitches. Work the last round of nine bead stitches without decreasing.

Small button: thread 48 beads. Starting by looping the thread (see pages 16 and 62) and work three bead stitches and nine bead stitches in the second round. In the third round work two bead stitches into every third stitch of the previous round = twelve beads. Work two more rounds with twelve beads, then push the bead shank into the work.

Work the next round in single crochet (UK double crochet) without beads, decreasing the stitches in pairs (see page 16).

Material

- rocailles, 2mm (¹/₁₆in) diameter (button A: 6 colours; button B: 4 colours)
- very fine crochet yarn in a matching colour
- 1 backing button or shank button, approximately 20mm (¾in) diameter
- cotton wadding/batting
- crochet hook size 11–10 (1–1.25mm)

How it's done

For button A, thread the beads as shown in the threading diagram. For button B, thread each round of beads in a different colour. The number of beads in a round is as shown in the diagram, i.e. 36, 36, 36, 30 etc. Crochet the button as described on pages 8–11. However, before working the back, you might want to sew one bead into the middle of the button with the starting thread, and then secure the thread (because of the rounded shape of the middle of the button the beads are further apart). Stuff the button with wadding/batting and shape it into a semi-sphere. Make the back.

Symbols

- ⚪ = white, opaque
- ⚫ = turquoise, opaque
- ◯ = light turquoise, opaque (crochet in spirals)
- ◓ = turquoise, transparent
- ◯ = light green, transparent
- ◓ = green, transparent
- ⚫ = anthracite, opaque

[18] = number of beads in this round

⚫⚫ = work 2 bead stitches into 1 stitch in the previous round (= increase 1)

Threading diagram for button A

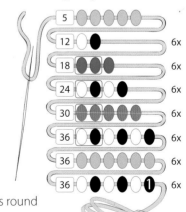

5		
12		6x
18		6x
24		6x
30		6x
36		6x
36		6x
36		6x

Material
- rocailles, 2mm (¹/₁₆in) diameter
- very fine crochet yarn in a matching colour
- shank button of the desired size
- crochet hook size 11–10 (1–1.25mm)

How it's done
The size chart shows the numbers of beads required. The figures are based on flat buttons. For the slightly rounded buttons in the illustrations, the crocheted item will fit better if one additional row is worked on the outside with the same number of beads as in the previous row. These figures are provided in brackets.

Thread beads of the same colour, each round in a different colour, or as per the diagrams for buttons C and D. You can also achieve terrific results with random combinations of buttons.

It's a good idea to mark the beginning of each round with a little piece of paper when you do the threading (see page 8). Once threaded, approximately 60–65 beads measure about 10cm (4in). Crochet the buttons as described on pages 8–11.

If working in plain or mixed beads, also increase six stitches in each row from row three. In row three, crochet two bead stitches in every second stitch, in row four in every third stitch, and in row five in every fourth stitch etc.

27 mm (1⅛in)

(possibly eighth round with 42 beads for domed buttons)
7th round: 42 beads

27mm (1in) diameter
167 or 209 beads

22 mm (¾in)

(possibly seventh round with 36 beads for domed buttons)
6th round: 36 beads
5th round: 30 beads

22mm (¾in) diameter
125 or 161 beads

16 mm (⅝in)

(possibly fifth round with 24 beads for domed buttons)
4th round: 24 beads

16mm (⅝in) diameter
59 or 83 beads

12 mm (½in)

(possibly fourth round with 18 beads for domed buttons)
3rd round: 18 beads
2nd round: 12 beads
1st round: 5 beads

12mm (½in) diameter
35 or
53 beads

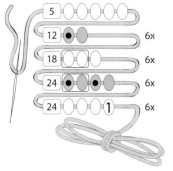

Threading diagram for button C
(crochet in rounds, see page 18 for symbols)

5
12   6x
18   6x
24   6x
24 1   6x

Threading diagram for button D
(crochet in spirals)

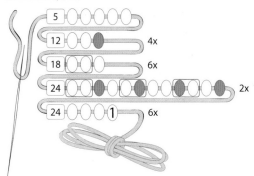

5
12   4x
18   6x
24   2x
24 1   6x

Squares

The principle is the same for crocheting squares as for crocheting in the round, except you increase differently, which is what produces corners and edges.

◉◉ CROCHETING SQUARES

Thread the beads in accordance with the instructions. Work eight chain stitches, then slip stitch into the first chain to make a ring and crochet one bead stitch into each stitch. End the round with one slip stitch in the first stitch of the round. Chain one stitch, then continue working the next round. Work the first bead stitch of the next round into the slip stitch at the end of the round, i.e. into the first stitch of the previous round.

1 Work the following rows in the same way. The diagonal stitch (green arrow) is the slip stitch at the end of the last row. The chain stitch to change rows (red arrow) is worked over it. The slip stitch at the end of the row (white arrow) is worked into the first stitch of the previous row.

2 At the corners, work three bead stitches into the corner stitches in the previous round. Unless indicated otherwise in the threading diagram, in row two work three bead stitches into every second stitch, in row three into every fourth stitch, in row five into every sixth stitch etc.

3 Increasing at the corners creates a square. With the larger buttons that are crocheted using shank buttons measuring approximately 22 x 22mm (¾ x ¾in), in the last round work two bead stitches into the corner stitches instead of three so that the beads lie firmly against the crochet. Then work one round of single crochets (UK double crochets) without beads and without increasing.

Secure the beginning of the thread and sew one bead into the middle of the button. Work the back as for the round buttons (see page 11).

TIP: If you have threaded too many beads or used one in the wrong colour, you can crush it with pliers to remove it. Push a needle through the bead, to protect the yarn and so as not to cut it with the broken bead. Put some paper towel around the pliers and the bead to catch the splinters.

If a bead is missing, work a single crochet (UK double crochet) in that place and sew the matching bead onto the spare stitch at the end.

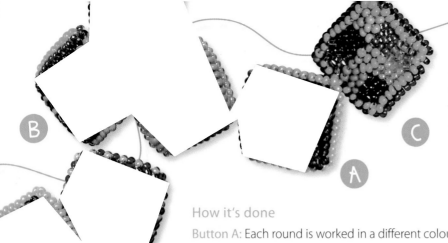

Materials (per button)

- rocailles, 2mm ($^1/_{16}$ in) diameter (for button A: 4–6 colours; for button B: 7 colours; for button C: 9 colours)
- very fine crochet yarn in a matching colour
- square shank button, approximately 22 x 22mm (¾ x ¾in)
- crochet hook size 11–10 (1–1.25mm)

How it's done

Button A: Each round is worked in a different colour. First thread the last row with forty-four beads, then continue with forty, thirty-two, twenty-four, sixteen and eight beads for rows one to five. As a variation, you can also alternate two colours for one or more rounds. Another option is to use one or more colours a number of times rather than just for one row. Crochet the button (see page 20).

Buttons B and C: Thread the beads as shown in the respective diagrams. Crochet the button (see page 20), increasing as indicated in the diagram.

Threading diagram for button B

Threading diagram for button C

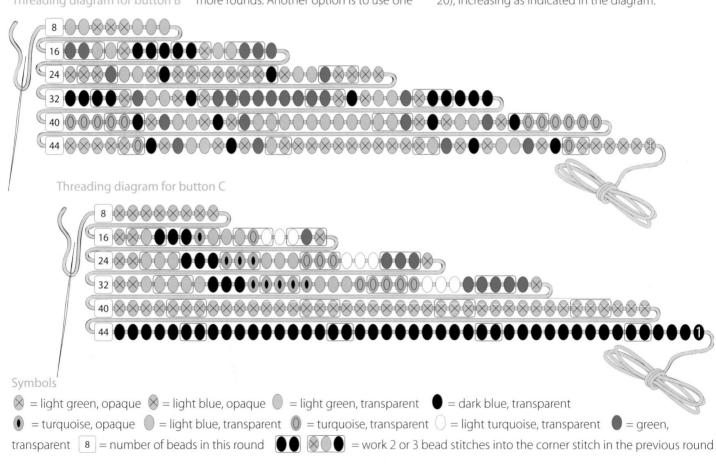

Symbols

⊗ = light green, opaque　⊗ = light blue, opaque　◯ = light green, transparent　● = dark blue, transparent
◉ = turquoise, opaque　◯ = light blue, transparent　◎ = turquoise, transparent　◯ = light turquoise, transparent　● = green, transparent　8 = number of beads in this round　●● ⊗⊗● = work 2 or 3 bead stitches into the corner stitch in the previous round

Cylinders

If you increase fewer stitches, you will end up with a cylinder rather than a circle or square. You can make necklaces and bracelets from cylinders – and you can also make toggle fastenings.

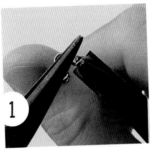

Toggled buttons crocheted from cylinders do not have a button shank on the inside so you have to crochet in a wire hook eye (see page 6) to attach the buttons. Hook-and-eye fastenings made of aluminium or stainless steel wire can be bent into place and are quick and easy to use.

BENDING A HOOK EYE

1 The easiest way to do this is with two pairs of pliers: use flat-nose pliers to grip the eye (the rounded bent part), and with the other pair bend the tiny hook eyes so they stand out at an angle of 90°.
2 Squeeze the neck of the eye gently to make it easier to work it into the crochet.

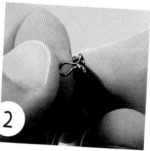

CROCHETING IN A HOOK EYE

3 The instructions on page 8 tell you where to put a piece of paper to mark the beginning of each round. Crochet as far as the marked place, then chain one and push the hook eye into the crochet with the large wire hoop facing outward.
Miss the next stitch (the hook eye will fill this gap), then continue working bead stitches as before.
4 In the next round, again work one bead stitch into the chain so that the number of stitches remains the same in each round. Continue crocheting according to the instructions. When you decrease, carefully stuff the button with wadding/batting (if instructed) without moving the hook eye on the inside.

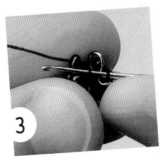

Materials (per button)

- rocailles, in one or two colours, 2mm ($^1/_{16}$in) diameter
- very fine crochet yarn in a matching colour
- 1 eye of a hook-and-eye fastening
- crochet hook size 11–10 (1–1.25mm)

  (The buttons look better if they are crocheted quite tightly.)

How it's done

Striped button: The cylinder is crocheted with nine stitches to a round, whereas the striped pattern has ten beads per repeat. This creates diagonal stripes.

Start by threading four light red/lilac beads, then forty-seven beads – alternating one light red /dark red or black / lilac bead. Later on you will work in the hook eye instead of the next dark red / lilac bead. Mark this place with a piece of paper (see page 8). Then start again with light red / black, and thread another forty-eight beads in alternating colours plus four light red / lilac beads. To start, crochet four bead stitches in a loop of thread (see pages 16 and 62). In the next round, work two bead stitches three times and three bead stitches once into each stitch in the previous round = nine beads. Continue in spirals without increasing to the marked place. Work in the hook eye (see page 23) and continue crocheting until only thirteen beads are left on the thread. In the next round, decrease two bead stitches together three times and three bead stitches together once = four stitches. Work one round with four bead stitches.

For the plain button, thread fifty-one beads, mark the place for the eye, and thread another fifty-two beads. Crochet the button as described above.

Materials (per button)

- rocailles in four colours, 2mm ($^1/_{16}$in) diameter
- very fine crochet yarn in a matching colour
- 1 eye of a hook-and-eye fastening
- cotton wadding/batting
- crochet hook size 11–10 (1–1.25mm)

How it's done

For the beginning, thread twenty-six beads in anthracite, then thread five repeats of eighteen stitches for the striped pattern (the diagram shows one repeat), and insert a paper marker after seventeen beads. For the next (sixth) repeat, replace the first bead with the marker for the hook eye, and start with two red beads. Repeat this to the end and thread four more repeats, then twenty-six beads in anthracite.

Start by crocheting four bead stitches in a loop (see pages 16 and 62). In the next round, crochet three bead stitches three times and two bead stitches once into each stitch in the previous round = eleven beads. Crochet eleven bead stitches in round three. In the following round, crochet two bead stitches into the first and then every other stitch = seventeen beads. Continue crocheting in spirals without increasing as far as the marker.

Work in the hook eye (see page 23) and continue to the next marker. In the following round, work the first and second and then every second and third bead stitch together to decrease = 11 stitches. Stuff the button with wadding/batting. Work one round in bead stitches and in the following round decrease three stitches together three times and two bead stitches together once = four stitches. If required, add a little more wadding/batting when you decrease. Work one more round of four bead stitches.

Threading diagram for one repeat of 18 beads

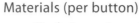

= orange, transparent   = lilac, transparent

= red, transparent   = anthracite, opaque

Material

- rocailles, 2mm (¹/₁₆ in) diameter
- very fine crochet yarn in a matching colour
- 1 eye of a hook-and-eye fastening (see page 23)
- cotton wadding /batting
- crochet hook size 11–10 (1–1.25mm)

How it's done

Thread 143 beads (approximately 22cm / 8¾ in). Crochet three bead stitches into a loop (see pages 16 and 62). Mark the beginning of the round with different coloured thread.

2nd round: work two bead stitches into every stitch = 6 beads.

3rd round: work two bead stitches into second every stitch = 9 beads.

4th round: work two bead stitches into every third stitch = 12 beads.

5th round: work two bead stitches into every fourth stitch = 15 beads.

6th round: work two bead stitches into every fifth stitch = 18 beads.

7th round: nine bead stitches, crochet in hook eye (see page 23), one chain to skip one stitch, eight bead stitches.

8th round: decrease every 5th and 6th bead stitch together = 15 stitches (see page 23).

9th round: decrease every fourth and fifth bead stitch together = 12 stitches. Stuff the button with wadding/batting, and add a little more over the following rows as required.

10th round: decrease every third and fourth bead stitch together = 9 stitches.

11th round: decrease every second and third bead stitch together = 6 stitches.

12th round: decrease two bead stitches together = 3 stitches.

13th round: work three slip stitches, then work in one bead as for the bead stitches in single crochet (UK double).

Materials (per button)

- rocailles, 2mm (¹/₁₆ in) diameter, in three shades of red and gold (see below)
- very fine crochet yarn in a matching colour
- 1 eye of a hook-and-eye fastening (see page 23)
- 1 book screw, 50mm (2in) long
- crochet hook size 11–10 (1–1.25mm)

How it's done

The diagram shows the beads that need to be threaded for one repeat. Thread twenty-four repeats, omitting the last bead in the twelfth repeat and instead mark the place for the hook eye with a piece of paper.

Work twelve chain stitches and join with a slip stitch. Continue working bead stitches in spirals, keeping an eye on the height of the cylinder: after twelve repeats, the work should measure about 25mm (1in) at the marker, i.e. halfway up the book screw. Work the hook eye in at the marker (see page 23). Continue working in spirals. Work the last bead in with one slip stitch, then cut off the thread, draw through and secure.

Push the sleeve nut of the book screw into the crocheted piece and secure on the other side with the screw.

Threading diagram for one repeat of thirteen beads

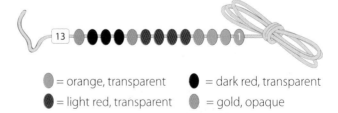

● = orange, transparent   ● = dark red, transparent
● = light red, transparent   ● = gold, opaque

Painted & embroidered

A basic sewing machine is ideal for embroidering circles, spirals and little boxes on your painted fabrics.

◉ PAINTING FABRIC

1 Set the fabric in an embroidery frame. Start with the lighter colours, then apply the darker ones. Colour an area that is a little bigger than the chosen button size. This will prevent any unwanted white areas around the edge of the button. Take the fabric out of the embroidery frame and iron on the wrong side, placing a piece of baking parchment under the fabric to protect your ironing board.

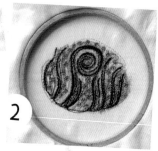

◉◉ EMBROIDERING

2 Set the fabric in the frame with embroidery fleece. If you put the fabric in the frame the wrong way round with the larger ring under the fabric and the small one on top, you can use an ordinary embroidery frame. Depending on the size of the fabric, you can also work with just the embroidery fleece or embroidery foil without a frame.

Lower or cover the feed dogs (refer to the instructions for your machine) and insert an embroidery or quilting foot.

Loosen the upper thread slightly so that the lower thread does not show on the front. Choose the lower thread in the matching colour, just to be on the safe side.

Sewing machine embroidery thread is best: it is a little thicker and shinier than normal sewing thread, and creates brighter results. With the fabric in the embroidery frame, you can move it freely under the sewing foot. The pre-drawn buttons are ideal for this technique. Make sure your stitches aren't too short.

A stitch length of 2–2.5mm (13 stitches per inch) will show the thread at its best. If you want to embroider areas and contours, the contours will be much clearer if you sew them at the end. It is also better to sew any special effects, such as lines in gold, after all the other colours.

TIP: Metallic yarns are not as strong as other yarns, and are also far more sensitive. If the yarn breaks frequently or starts to fray, you might need to check the needle. You can also buy special needles for metallic yarns, which have a bigger eye than normal needles. Sometimes it can help to loosen the upper tension a little.

The backing

A split backing makes it easy to turn the button right side out, stuff it and sew up the turning opening – a neat solution!

● SEWING THE BACKING

Either sew a plain uncovered button into the backing (yellow backing fabric) or work the back with a simple seam in the middle and a split ring to secure the button (pink backing fabric). Each backing version will consist of two rectangles of fabric.

Cut out two fabric rectangles about 2cm (¾in) longer than the button (= side edge) and half as wide as the finished button plus 4cm (1½in) seam allowance (= top and bottom edge).

1 Uncovered button: On each rectangle, iron one side edge 1cm (³/₈in) to the wrong side. Place the white coat button on the cut edge as illustrated, and draw the outline on the fold. Prepare both pieces like this, and sew along the drawn line.

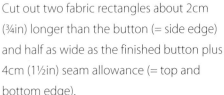

2 + 3 for either version: Place the pieces together with the right sides facing and sew up the middle seam on the sides, leaving an opening in the middle that is a little smaller than the finished button. Do not pick up the fold on the version with the white coat button. Place the rectangles on the top of the button and mark the opening.

4 Iron the seam allowance apart. Place the back on the front of the button with the right sides together. If you hold the pieces against the light, you can check that the seam and opening are in the middle. Sew the two pieces together in the desired button shape. Trim the seam allowances back to 5mm (¼in).

5 On the rounded section, snip into the seam allowance, leaving short gaps between, to just before the seam. Turn the button piece right side out. Push the seam to the outside with your fingers.

6 Place the button on the interfacing, draw around, and cut out 3mm (¹/₈in) smaller than the button on all sides.

7 Cut a hole in the middle of the interfacing to make it looser. Push the interfacing into the button. Stuff the button with a little wadding/batting if required. Push the uncovered button into the pre-sewn pocket and sew up the opening with fell stitches.

For the plain back, sew on the split ring.

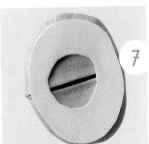

Materials (per button)

- light, finely woven fabric to colour
- wax-based fabric crayons
- sewing machine embroidery thread
- embroidery fleece
- embroidery frame
- baking parchment
- rocailles, 2mm (1/16in) diameter (if required)

For the button back: :

- strong interfacing
- cotton wadding/batting
- uncovered button or split ring button (alternatively, use any type of button that can be covered)

How it's done

The buttons on this page are all shown actual size.
Use them as the base for your own ideas or as templates or patterns (for more information see pages 26 and 28). Part of the charm of these buttons lies in the lines not being quite straight as nothing is drawn with a ruler.
If possible, finish the embroidered lines on the edge of the button (along the seam allowance) rather than in the middle so that the ends of the threads do not show on the surface.

Sew any beads on at the end. Sew one or two small stitches after sewing on three or four beads so that the beads will not come loose too easily. On the square button, the embroidered fabric is worked as for the graffiti buttons (see pages 46–48).

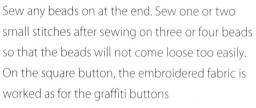

Drawing patterns

Freehand embroidery is like drawing with a sewing machine. Combining fabrics, textures and yarn colours creates a wide range of designs and patterns.

⬤ TRANSFERRING PATTERNS

1 There are lots of ways to transfer patterns to fabric or draw the motif of your choice. Basic drawings with just a few lines for orientation can be drawn onto the fabric by hand in chalk, water-soluble marker pen or with powdered chalk and a chalk roller. Remember, though, that chalk brushes off quite easily.

⬤ TRACING PATTERNS

2 Trace more complex patterns directly onto lighter fabrics. This can be done by projecting the preliminary drawing with a light box onto the fabric (or you can use a piece of glass, e.g. from a picture frame, with a light below it). Trace the drawing with marker pens. For darker fabrics, use water-soluble fleece. Place the translucent fleece on the original and trace. Put the fleece on the fabric and sew the motif, then wash the fleece out in water.

Marker pens (which look like colouring pens) have the advantage of not running on the fleece. If you are using very light fabrics and threads, check first to make sure that the lines of the preliminary drawing can be washed out. Note, though, that the lines are usually covered by the sewing.

⬤ PRINTING PATTERNS

3 A printer will provide a very clear pattern. Back the thin fleece with freezer paper so you can print directly on it. However, be warned, a printer is not designed for this purpose. Although lots of crafters use this option, there is always a risk of damaging the printer.

Felt backings

Be inspired by felt fibre backings and create beautiful patterns and flowing colours for your buttons.

⊙ FELTING A BACKGROUND

1 Use felting wool to create sewing backgrounds with beautiful flowing colours. You will need felting wool (ideally combed), a dry felting needle and a felt base.

Wool fabric is best because the fibres are firmly anchored in the dense, rough fabric. Place the felt fibres on the felt base, then start by gently rubbing the felting needle all over the fibres in the fabric, and then gradually build up the pressure. This will gradually produce a fuzz on the back of the fabric.

For non-detachable buttons or buttons on smooth, loosely woven fabrics, be sure to wet felt the felt fibres on both sides of the fabric. Soak the fibres in hot, soapy water and rub together to felt them. Work very gently at first using small movements until the fibres have felted and can no longer slip. Now increase the pressure and use bigger movements.

2 Sew over the felt surface. Small circles, polka dot patterns, zigzags and spirals are just a few examples of what you can do. If the felt fibres are pushed into the fabric with a felting needle, the sewn stitches need to be worked close together in order to prevent the fibres from being pulled out when doing up and undoing the buttons. Then work the back (see page 28).

Lace and printed fabrics

3 Lace or printed fabrics also make good bases for sewing because they already include the pattern.

If you are using lace, back with a different fabric and then set the two in the frame. Then sew over or complete the areas, contours etc. that are indicated by the lace.

4 To mark the button outlines on the back, sew a line at the desired distance from the motif plus a seam allowance of 1mm ($^1/_{32}$ in), ideally in a contrasting colour. Then work the back (see page 28), sewing the edge of the button close to the sewn marker line.

TIP: Fragile buttons will last longer if the button holes are big enough for the buttons to slide through without having to be forced.

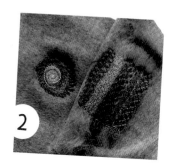

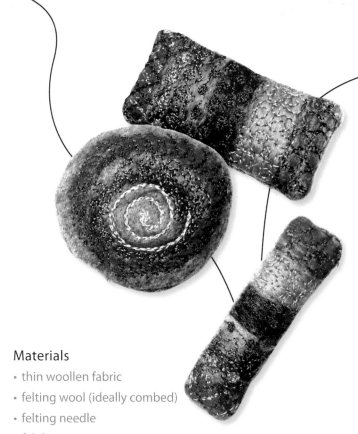

Materials

- lace fabric
- matching fabric for base/back
- machine threads in matching colours
- cotton wadding/batting
- strong interfacing
- shank button or split ring button
- beads if desired

How it's done

Set the lace and background fabrics in a frame as described on page 32. Sew over the contours and areas. Work the back. Turn the button right side out and stuff (see page 28).

If you wish, you can add satin stitching or French knots e.g. in gold (see page 38).

You can also sew beads into the middle of the flowers.

Materials

- thin woollen fabric
- felting wool (ideally combed)
- felting needle
- felt base
- machine threads in matching colours
- cotton wadding/batting
- strong interfacing
- shank button or split ring button

How it's done

Work the felt fibres into the fabric as described on page 32 and embroider the top of the button. If you are making square buttons, perhaps work a large piece so you can make several of them. Work the back, then turn the button right side out and stuff it (see page 28). With longer buttons, it is sufficient to stuff the buttons firmly; the interfacing is not necessarily required.

Materials

- fabric for embroidering (some relatively firm fabrics; a few layers of a transparent fabric and a firm base fabric is recommended)
- machine threads in matching colours
- chalk or marker pen
- embroidery frame
- embroidery fleece
- water-soluble fleece, if desired
- cotton wadding/batting
- strong interfacing
- shank button or split ring button

How it's done

Transfer the preliminary drawings onto the fabric or fleece (see page 30). Set the fabric in an embroidery frame and embroider the top of the button (see page 26).

Either sew a fabric backing (see page 28) or put the buttons on a button blank (see pages 43–44).

Materials

- fabric for embroidering
- coloured fabric scraps for appliqués
- machine sewing thread in matching colours
- chalk or marker pen
- double-sided iron-on fleece
- embroidery fleece
- cotton wadding/batting
- strong interfacing
- shank button or split ring button

How it's done

Place the iron-on fleece on the pattern with the fabric side up and draw circles for the appliqués. Put all the circles of the same colour that you want to cut out close together.

Iron the fleece onto the wrong sides of the various fabrics and cut the circles out precisely. Pull off the protective paper. Place the circles on the base fabric and iron on.

Sew the decorative lines first, then set the stitch to zigzag (still using the embroidery foot and with the feed dogs down) and appliqué the fabric circles.

Either sew a fabric backing (see page 28) or put the buttons on a button blank (see pages 43–44). Make the buttons big enough for an edge of the background fabric to be visible.

Templates

Appliqué circles

Felt buttons

There's something magical about the texture of felt – these felt buttons feel fantastic and they look great too.

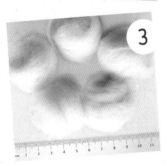

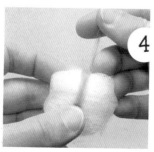

Material

- felting wool in natural and various colours (ideally combed)
- soap
- split rings, approximately 5mm (¼in) diameter
- rocailles, 2mm (¹⁄₁₆in) diameter
- embroidery thread in matching colours
- sharp embroidery needle
- if desired, bubble wrap or bamboo mat

◉ FELTING SPHERES

1 Cover your working area with bubble wrap or a bamboo mat and prepare some hot, soapy water. You will need to add more hot water and soap as required.
With their rough surfaces, bubble wrap or bamboo place mats make good felting bases that you can roll the felt balls over after felting the outer layer.

2 Pull off a number of clumps of wool, each in the same size. Tie a knot at the end of one strand and wrap the wool around it to make a sphere.

3 It's a good idea to make all the balls at the same time. The finished balls will be about one-third bigger than what you started with. Felt a sample ball to obtain the correct button size.

4 Pull a few fibres off the coloured felt and wrap around the ball. It only takes a few fibres to make eye-catching lines.

  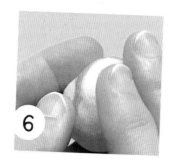 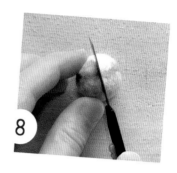

5 + 6 Dip the sphere in the soapy water. When you first start, gently stroke the surface of the ball until the outer layer just starts to felt and has a certain degree of firmness. To achieve even results, it is essential that you start out by felting slowly using tiny movements and no pressure.

7 Once you have felted the outer layer, increase the pressure and use bigger circles. Keep dipping the ball in the hot water, and squeeze it occasionally to make sure that the water gets right to the centre of it.

You can make a nugget as an alternative to a ball. Flatten the felt ball after felting it, and rub it in your hand until it has the desired firmness.

8 When the ball is about half to one-third as big as at the beginning, halve it with a cutter so that the coloured lines are roughly in the middle over the hemisphere. Continue felting the hemispheres in your hand until the cut is rounded.

☺ HAND STITCHES

9 Satin stitch: A basic stitch that creates terrific effects. Lots of tiny satin stitches worked evenly over an area are also called

bourdon stitches. Pull the needle out in the desired spot and insert it again 1–3mm (1/32–1/8 in) beside that spot and guide the needle straight to the next exit point. On fixed buttons, you might prefer to guide the needle to the underside of the button first, and then on to the next stitch.

10 Daisy stitch: Pull the needle out at the first insertion point and insert it again. Pull it out at the second insertion point and loop the thread under the needle. Draw the thread through, put the loop in the right position, and insert the needle at the second insertion point again. This time, though, on the other side of the loop so that it is secured in place with a tiny stitch. Pull the needle out again at the beginning of the next stitch.

11 + 12 French knot: Pull the needle out at the desired point, then gently pull on the thread and wrap it around the needle one to three times, close to the exit point. Insert the needle close to or into the exit point. Pull the thread through the loops on the needle and through the fabric. Keep the thread taut so that the loops on the needle stay firmly in place and make a knot. When embroidering the felt buttons, attach a split ring to the back of the button to use when sewing on the button.

  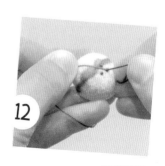

Hand embroidered

First paint the base, then embroider the contours by hand. The result will be striking floral embroidered buttons.

Materials

- linen or cotton cambric in white
- fabric pens in yellow, orange, green, blue, red and magenta
- embroidery thread in matching colours
- embroidery frame
- sharp embroidery needle
- button blanks to cover, approximately 27mm (1 1/16 in) diameter

😊 SEWING BY HAND

1 Set the fabric in the frame (small ring on top, large ring under the fabric), then place on the templates on page 42 and colour in the desired areas.

2 For finer outlines, start by drawing the contours with a thin fabric pen, then fill in the area with a thicker one. For adjoining areas, let the first colour dry before applying the second one. Leave enough space between the drawings for a circle of 45mm (1¾in) diameter for the round heads, and one of 40mm (1½in) diameter for the squares. Embroider the coloured areas in various stitches (satin stitch and French knots, see page 38).

3 Backstitch: This is sewn from right to left. Pull the needle out in the desired spot, then move it along 3mm (⅛ in) to the left and insert it, then pull it out again. Pull the thread through.

4 Move the needle 3mm (⅛ in) back to the right, and insert it in the last point again. Move to the left under the fabric, and pull it out 3mm (⅛ in) to the left of the last point of exit. Keep repeating this sequence.

5 Chain stitch: This is worked from the bottom to the top. Draw the needle out at the desired point and pull the thread up.

★ Insert the needle in the same place again, then pull it out approximately 3mm (⅛ in) further up, winding a loop around the needle.

6 + 7 Pull the thread through and make the first chain link. Repeat from ★. Cover the buttons (see pages 43–44).

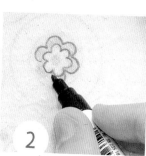
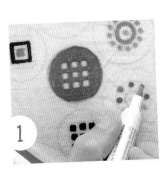
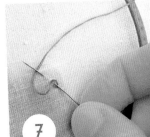
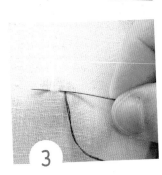
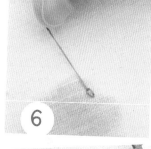
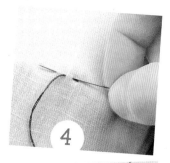
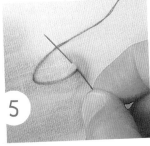

Templates

The red lines indicate the area that will be visible on the finished button.

Covering buttons

If you like, you can make your own button covers, however, you can also buy button blanks that can easily be covered.

Material
- button blanks of the desired size
- marker pen
- flat-nose pliers
- stencil film if desired
  (or left-over transparent wrapping)

How it's done

1 The packaging for the button blanks should include information on the required fabric. For embroidered buttons (or if choosing a particular fabric cut-out), it is easier to work with a transparent template that you can cut out in accordance with the information on the packaging. If only cardboard is available, simply cut a hole in the middle of the template to position the circle correctly.

2 Cut out the circle and place around the top of the button. Check the position of the motif.

3 Using the pliers, draw the fabric over the button on four sides, and push over the hooks. Check the position of the motif again.

4 Draw the fabric firmly over the edge so that it is lying smoothly and evenly on the button.

5 Push the underside of the button onto the back until it clicks into place.

6 The button you can see here was sewn freehand (see page 26). All you need as the preliminary drawing are a few circles for division. Measure the button blank to establish the diameter of the circle that will be seen on the front of the finished button. The rest of the pattern is created directly under the sewing machine.

Old into new

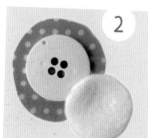

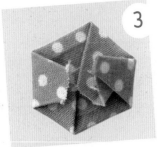

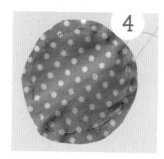

Although this technique requires a little more effort, it can give even the shabbiest button a new lease on life.

◉ COVERING OLD BUTTONS

1 Draw a circle on the fabric with a diameter about twice that of the button. Cut out the circle.

2 Cut out another circle about 3–5mm (⅛–¼in) bigger than the button for the back of the button. If required, cut a button-sized circle out of fleece so that the surface of the button is smooth.

3 Fold over the edges of the circle for the back and iron them to the wrong side to make a hexagon. The hexagon should be a little smaller than the button.

4 Tack the circle for the front using a needle and double thread.

5 Put the button (with the volume fleece, if desired) into the circle and pull the ends of the thread together so that the fabric encloses the button. Knot the ends of the threads and secure.

6 Place the button back on the front and sew on using blind stitches. Push the needle out on the edge of the back, and insert it in the fabric just above that point. Then move the needle to the left under the fabric, and pull it out on the edge. Keep repeating this sequence.

7 This is what the back of the finished button will look like. The button is simply sewn on through the fabric. Alternatively, you could crochet a back. Crochet rounds one to four (see page 62), and push a hook eye (see page 23) into the opening before tightening the loop.

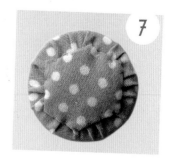

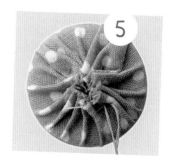

Materials

- old button
- marker pen
- sewing needle
- firm sewing thread
- volume fleece, if required
- covering fabric

Cartoon buttons

A trendy illustrated button will look good on a denim jacket or bag. And if you don't like embroidering, you can draw the patterns yourself with a fabric pen.

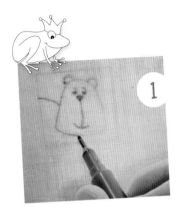

Materials

- white linen, 15 x 10cm (6 x 4in) per button
  (linen batiste is best for tracing patterns)
- strong iron-on interfacing
- iron
- sewing thread in black and white
- embroidery thread in bright pink (for the flower)
- tear-out embroidery fleece
- aluminium wire, 1mm ($^1/_{32}$in) diameter
- flat-nose pliers
- wire cutters
- water-soluble marker pen
- punch pliers
- rotating cutter, cutting mat, cutting ruler

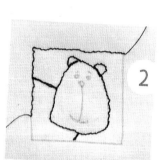

How it's done

1 Place the fabric on the pattern (see patterns on page 49), and use a light box to project your image (a light under an empty picture frame glass will also do the trick). Draw over the lines with the marker pen.

2 Set up your sewing machine for freehand embroidery. Fit the embroidery or quilting foot and lower or cover the feed dogs. Refer to the manufacturer's instructions for further information. Use black sewing thread

3 Here is one possible sewing sequence: sew two to three stitches in one place before stopping and at the beginning and end of the short lines (the double lines are easy to see, and should be positioned evenly, i.e. sew both connecting lines to the ears, or the two ears, double). Always sew double on the outer frame. For the flower (see photo on right), first embroider the area in pink and then follow the contours in black.

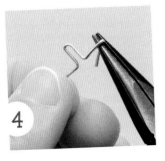

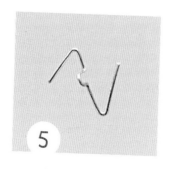

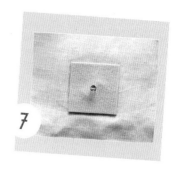

4 + 5 Cut 4cm (1½in) pieces of aluminium wire. First fold the wire in half to form a shank in the middle. Bend the ends outward to the angle as shown in the picture. The shank should be about 5mm (¼in) high.

6 Use the roller cutter to cut out two squares of interfacing measuring 3.25 x 3.25cm (1 ⅜ x 1 ⅜in) for each button. Draw the diagonals on one square to mark the middle. Use the punch pliers to make a 3–4mm (⅛–¼in) hole in the middle. The shank needs to fit through this hole. Iron the square without the hole onto the wrong side of the embroidery. The square should just cover the embroidered frame. Trim the top and bottom of the fabric 1.5cm (½in) from the interfacing, and the sides 2.5cm (1in) from the interfacing.

7 Place the shank on the square so that it is parallel to the top edge of the fabric. Put the square with the hole over the shank and iron onto the first square. Iron the damp cloth around the shank a few times.

8 Iron the top and bottom edge of the fabric back around the edge of the interfacing, making the sides a little wider so that the strip is narrower to the outside (see image). Then iron the side edges back.

9 Open out the side edges and tighten the cut edges that meet at the centre with satin stitch, and secure (inserting the needle in the right side of the fabric, guide the needle to the left under the fabric and pull it through).

10 Fold the raw edges of the sides to the wrong side so that the cut edges meet at the shank. Secure the sides with fell stitches. Secure the thread on the inside, then push the needle through the edge that is to be attached. Insert the needle in the fabric close to the exit point, and guide the needle to the left through the fabric. Pull the needle out about 2mm (¹⁄₁₆in) further along on the edge, and insert it again just above the edge and guide the needle to the left. Any stitches that show will be tiny.

11 This is what the back of the finished button will look like.

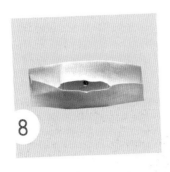

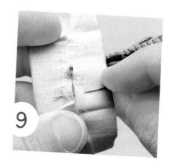

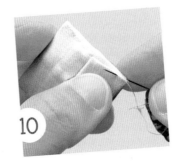

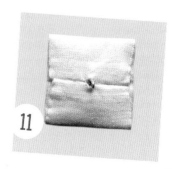

Templates

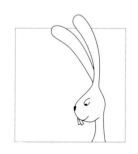

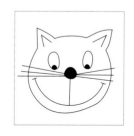

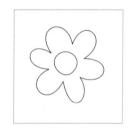

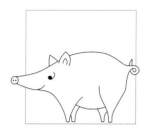

Roll-ups

Book screws can do so much more than just bind folders and papers together. They can also be wrapped in tiny fabric scraps or pretty velvet ribbons.

Materials
- fabric scraps or patterned ribbons
- iron-on fleece, if required (to join several ribbons together)
- book screws of the required height
- double-sided sticky tape for textiles
- split rings

How's it done

1 Cut a strip of fabric to double the height of the book screw plus 1–2mm ($^1/_{32}$–$^1/_{16}$ in). Iron the two cut edges over to the middle of the strip with the wrong sides facing so that the fabric is doubled all over. It is important to make sure that the fabric thickness is the same all over for when you wrap the strip around the book screw later on. Line narrow strips up close together and iron fleece onto the wrong side to join them together. Trim the strips to 9.5cm (3¾in).

2 Stick the adhesive tape onto the back of the strip, taking care to cover the cut sides of the fabric.

3 Screw the book screw together. Pull the backing off the adhesive tape and wrap the strip firmly around the screw.

4 Trim off any excess fabric and fold the end 0.5cm (¼in) over to the wrong side. Place a small piece of adhesive tape onto the fold and press down firmly. Secure the strip with fell stitches. Pull the needle through on the edge, then insert it just above the edge and guide the needle through the fabric and slightly to the left. Insert it in the edge again and work the next stitch.

5 Sew a split ring on at the middle of the seam. First secure the thread with two or three stitches, then push through the ring and the fabric a few times.

6 Wind the thread around the stitching at the bottom of the ring a few times and secure the thread with a few stitches. Sew up the second half of the seam.

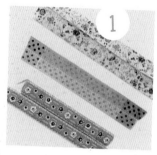

Knotted

Whether used as a fastening on a kimono or tunic, the "monkey's fist" knot always looks good. Once you have got the hang of it, you can make a whole new row of buttons in minutes!

Materials (per knot)

- Satin cord, 2mm (1/16 in) diameter, 1.6m (63in)
- Plastic bead, 12mm (1/2in) diameter

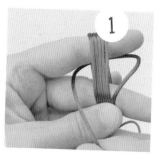

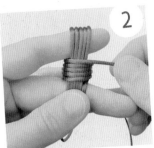

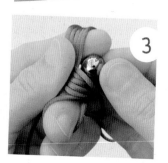

How it's done

1 Leave about 10cm (4in) of one end of the satin cord hanging and hold it with the thumb and ring finger of your left hand. Slightly spread your index and middle fingers, and wrap the cord around them five times. Move the free end of the cord behind the wraps to the left and then between your index and middle fingers at the front.

2 Wind the cord five times around the vertical wraps from left to right. The resulting space should be big enough for the bead.

3 Push the bead into the space, holding the wraps tight with your thumb.

4 Carefully move the wraps a little to the front with your index and middle fingers, making the openings bigger.

Thread the free end of the cord through the opening over the ball and the horizontal wraps, working from front to back.

5 + 6 Continue from back to front under the ball, and wrap five times around the horizontal wraps.

7 Pull all the wraps tight. Start with the first wraps that are still very loose, and wind each one individually around the ball from the beginning of the cord to the end of each wrap.

8 This is what the finished ball will look like – called a "monkey's fist". If the cord and/or ball have different diameters, this will change the number of wraps required. The knot makes a very pretty fastening.

To attach the knot as a fastening, sew an underflap onto the left edge of the closure, and include the ball knots at the beginning of the seam. You might want to zigzag the two cords next to the seam on the underflap (see photo, left). Sew loops of the appropriate size to the right side of the closure.

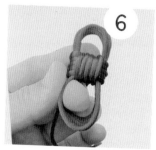

Macramé fastening

Macramé cords are usually crocheted together to make little doilies. However, they are also delightful sewn together as fastenings.

◉ CROCHET MACRAMÉ CORD

1 Start by crocheting three chain stitches. Insert the hook into the second chain (red arrow), then into the first chain (green arrow). Draw yarn through the first two loops on the hook. Draw yarn through the remaining two loops on the hook.

2 Insert hook in the three loops at the bottom (see image).

3 Turn the work around so that the loops are at the top of the hook. Draw yarn through the first two loops on the hook. Draw yarn through the remaining two loops on the hook.

4 Insert hook through the two loops on the right edge of the work (see arrows). Turn the work around again and work the loops on the hook as described above. Continue working step 4.

Materials

- very fine crochet yarn
- plastic bead, 15mm (½in) diameter
- crochet hook no. 1.25 (US 10)

Crochet diagram

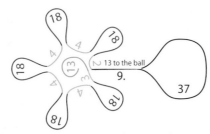

How it's done

Two rows of the macramé cord will make up a loop at the edge. Crochet one cord with 170 loops and one with 137. Crochet the ball onto the shorter cord (without cutting off the thread). Crochet two chain stitches and work nine single crochet (UK double crochet) into the first chain. Bring the cord forward over the stitch circle and close the round with one slip stitch into the first stitch so that the cord is on the inside of the round. Mark the beginning of the round with contrasting thread and continue working in spirals (inserting the hook in the back loop of the stitch).

In round two, work two single crochet (UK double crochet) into each stitch = eighteen stitches. In round three, work single crochet (UK double crochet) without increasing, in round four work two single crochet (UK double crochet) into every third stitch = twenty-four stitches. Work rounds five and six without increasing. In round seven decrease every third and fourth stitch together, pushing the bead onto the crochet work = eighteen stitches. In rounds eight and nine, decrease the second and third stitches together = twelve/eight stitches. Cut the yarn, pull through, and when sewing up pull the opening together and close.

Sew the outer loops together at the colour transitions in the drawing. The numbers indicate which loop is to be sewn on. First sew the cord together at the green/red transitions, then sew on the cord end at the middle and finally sew on the loop or the end with the ball.

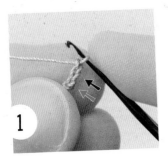

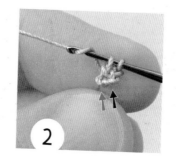

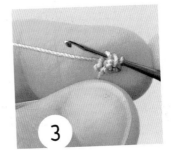

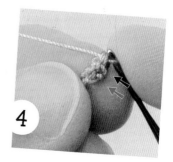

Sewing cords

Find the matching button to go with any knitted item. All you need to do is combine your knitting yarn with a few yarn remnants and...hey presto! – you have the perfect button.

● SEWING CORDS

1 Cut equal lengths of various yarns (you can also achieve terrific results with gold and other metallic yarns). Lower or cover the feed dogs (refer to the instructions for your machine) and insert an embroidery or quilting foot. Set to the widest zigzag stitch. Place the yarns under the sewing foot, twisting them slightly to make a round cord. Make sure that the needle always goes in to the left and right sides of the yarns when sewing.

2 The tension of the sewing thread determines what the cord will look like. In this picture, the cords have both been made of the same yarns, however, the top one was oversewn in turquoise and metallic turquoise, and the bottom one in pink.

3 You can add tiny patterns to a cord that has already been sewn. Sew over a small section in a tight zigzag, then change to straight stitch and sew 1–2cm (³⁄₈–³⁄₄in) along the middle of the cord. Then sew a small section in zigzag again.

To create a different effect, change the stitch length, i.e. sew very tight stitches and then change to ones with larger gaps between them. This creates different colour shades in the cord. The more you sew over the cord, the denser and stronger it will be.

● SEWING YARNS ON FABRIC

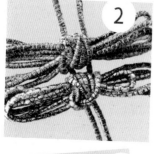

4 Instead of making loose cords, you can also sew slightly twisted yarns straight onto fabric. It's best to set the fabric in an embroidery frame for this, then place the bundled yarns on it and sew a few stitches at the beginning to secure. Then sew on the yarns in your choice of pattern with freehand zigzag stitches. Use the fabric to cover button blanks (see pages 43–44). You can also sew on some beads if you like.

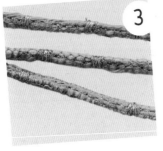

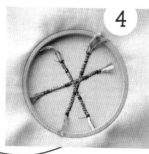

Cord buttons

There are many things you can use the monkey's fist knot for. For instance, by simply pulling the cord differently at the end, you can make buttons in different shapes.

Materials (per button)

- homemade cord, 1.6m (63in)
- sewing needle with matching thread
- split ring
- Version A: plastic bead or wooden ball, 12mm (½in) diameter
- Version B: decorative bead, approximately 8mm (³/₈in) diameter

How it's done

1 Version A: Make a monkey's fist knot (see page 52), but don't pull the wraps too tight. Carefully push the wraps apart at an intersection and push the ball out. Take care to move the wraps as little as possible.

2 Flatten the knot, leaving the hole at the bottom.

3 If necessary, pull the threads through to the back with a crochet hook.

4 Sew through the knot several times to make it stronger. Sew the split ring to the back.

5 Version B: Make a monkey's fist knot (see page 52) without a ball. Make sure that the vertical and horizontal wraps in the final step are all evenly tied.

To tighten the knot, just pull the first wraps that are standing out. Follow the cord from the protruding beginning to the last overhanging wrap before the horizontal wraps start. Start at this point and tighten the wraps towards the beginning.

6 This is what the finished knot will look like. Sew through the knot several times to make it stronger. Sew the split ring onto the back and, if you like, add a decorative bead onto the front.

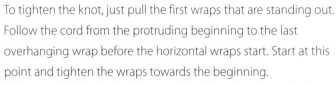

Materials

- homemade cord, approximately 80cm (31½in)
- pink rocailles, 2.6mm (¹¹⁄₃₂in) diameter
- sewing needle and thread
- plastic grid button, 38mm (1½in) diameter

How it's done

Push the start of the cord through the front and the middle opening in the button grid, and secure on the back with a few stitches. Wrap the cord around the middle of the front in three spirals, connecting the rounds to each other and to the button. Then lay the loops and again sew to the button and surrounding loops. Sew a bead into the middle of each loop. After the final loop, feed the end of the cord to the back through a button opening and secure.

Materials

- yarn scraps
- machine threads in matching colours
- self-adhesive tear-out embroidery fleece
- strong sewable iron-on interfacing
- split ring
- sewing needle
- cutter, embroidery frame, punch pliers
- mother-of-pearl discs and rocailles (optional)

How it's done

Sew the cords (see page 56). Set the embroidery fleece in an embroidery frame. Carefully slit the protective paper in the middle with the cutter and tear, leaving a sticky area that is a little bigger than you want the button to be. Stick the cord to the fleece in your chosen pattern, hiding the beginning and end of the cord under the arranged cord. Place the button shape down but without pushing it into place. Cut the cord to the required length. Lift the cord off the fleece, push the end of the cord under it and press down on the arranged cord.

Machine sew a few stitches over the cord. Cut out a piece of interfacing that is about 1mm (¹⁄₃₂in) smaller all round than the button. Punch a little hole in the middle to make it easier to sew the beads and button on later.

Iron the interfacing onto the back. Continue sewing over the front. Tear off the embroidery fleece and sew the split ring onto the back. Push the needle through the whole button and secure the front. Sew the bead and mother-of-pearl disc to the top of the button.

Flower power

All you need is an old pair of jeans. Denim can be quite tough and it will require a bit of patience to fray the edges properly, but it'll take no time at all to sew on the peace sign and smileys.

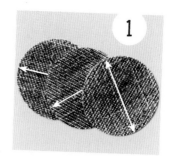

Materials

- denim or other fabric scraps
- button blanks
- sewing machine embroidery yarn
- water-soluble marker pen
- if desired, pliers and a hard brush (vegetable or nail brush)

How it's done

1 Cut two or three circles the size of your desired button and place them on top of each other with the grain on each circle facing a different way (see arrows).

2 Draw your chosen motif into the middle of one of the circles. If you prefer, you can also transfer the motif to water-soluble fleece (see page 30) and place that on the circles. Place the circles neatly on a piece of fabric that is big enough to cover the button. Sew the motif onto the middle of the circle.

3 Cover the button (see pages 43–44) and fray the edges of the circles. This is best done by separating the threads with a needle or using pliers to catch the ends of the threads and pulling them out. If you are using a thinner fabric, you might find it easier to moisten it and rub a hard brush over the edge to fray it.

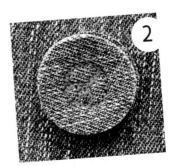

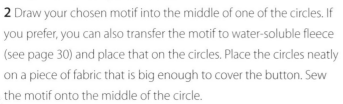

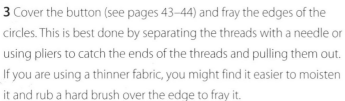

Crocheted buttons

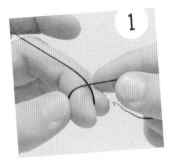

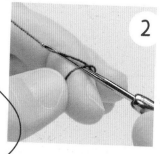

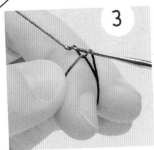

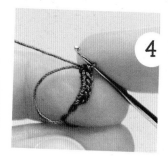

Try sewing these onto cards to make the perfect home-made gift.

⊙ LOOP TECHNIQUE

1 The stitches in the first round will be crocheted in a loop: wrap a loop around the middle finger of your left hand, and hold the end of it with the ring finger of the same hand.

2 Push the hook under the loop and pull one loop through, still holding on to the end of the yarn.

3 Work one chain, i.e. draw another loop through the loop on the hook.

4 Next, crochet six single crochet (UK double) of the first round, insert the hook under the loop and draw yarn through so you have two loops on the hook. Then draw a loop through the two loops on the hook. End the first round with one slip stitch in the first single crochet (UK double crochet).

When changing colours after the first round, work the slip stitches in the new colour. Work one chain stitch to change to second row. Work two single crochet (UK double crochet) into each stitch in the previous round, inserting the hook in the back loop only = twelve stitches. End the round with one slip stitch into the first single crochet (UK double crochet) (not into the chain stitch). Tighten the loop after the second round. Start each following round with one chain stitch. In the third round, work one single crochet (UK double crochet), then two single crochet (UK double crochet) into one stitch in the previous round = eighteen stitches. In the fourth round, work two single crochet (UK double crochet) into stitch = twenty-four stitches. In the fifth round, work two single crochet (UK double crochet) into every fourth stitch = thirty stitches. In the sixth round, increase in every fifth stitch, and in the seventh round in every sixth stitch = forty-two stitches.

Start the next round on the back of the button. Secure yarn and place the shank button on the back of the work. Working in spirals (no chain between rounds), decrease two single crochet (UK double crochet) together (see page 11).

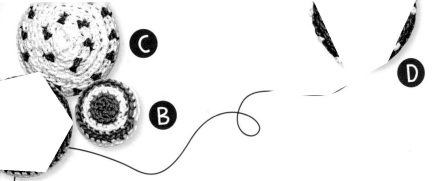

Materials

- very fine crochet yarn in white and magenta
- crochet hook size 10–8 (1.25–1.5mm)
- shank buttons, approximately 27mm (1 1/16in) diameter and 16mm (5/8in) diameter
- sharp embroidery needle

How it's done

Button A: Crochet the first to seventh rounds (see page 62). Start with white and alternate the colour at the end of each round. Work the slip stitch in the new colour at the end of the round. Work the back in white (see page 62).

Button B: as with button A, but start with magenta and work only five rounds for the front, then insert the little shank button and work the back in white (see page 62).

Button C: Crochet the first to seventh rounds (see page 62). Start with white, and in the third round work one stitch in magenta after the increase. Finish the previous stitch (= increase) in magenta. Finish the next stitch in magenta with white. In the sixth round, again start coloured stitches in magenta. Work every third (= stitch after increase) and sixth stitch as described in magenta. Work the back in white (see page 62).

Button D: Crochet the first to seventh rounds in magenta (see page 62). Increase the loop on the hook, but do not cut. Sew French knots (see page 38) in white. The rounds and increases serve as points of orientation when arranging the stitches. Secure the ends of the white threads and the starting thread, then insert the shank button and crochet the back in magenta (see page 62).

Materials

- very fine crochet yarn in orange, blue, light green and magenta
- crochet hook size 10–8 (1.25–1.5mm)
- shank button, approximately 27mm (1 1/16in) diameter
- sharp embroidery needle

How it's done

Cut off 60–70cm (23½–27½in) of the blue yarn for embroidering, and set aside. Crochet first to seventh rounds (see page 62), starting with blue. Crochet the third round in orange, the fourth and fifth in magenta, then one round in light green and one in orange. When changing colours, work the slip stitch at the end of the round in the new colour. Work the following round in blue with picots. Join the blue yarn at the end of the round with one slip stitch, ★ work three chain stitches, one single crochet (UK double crochet) in the first of the three chain stitches, miss one stitch, and work one single crochet (UK double crochet) into the front loop of the next stitch. Repeat from ★. Close the round with one slip stitch in the first blue chain.

Increase the loop on the hook, but do not cut the blue yarn. Secure the yarn ends and then sew French knots in blue and magenta (see page 38). Insert the shank button and crochet the back in blue (see page 62), working the first round in the back loops of the stitches in the seventh round in orange so that the blue picots protrude over the side of the button.

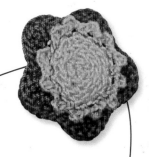

Materials

- very fine crochet yarn in orange, blue, light green and magenta
- crochet hook size 10–8 (1.25–1.5mm)
- shank button, approximately 27mm (1 1/16 in) diameter
- sharp embroidery needle

How it's done

Crochet the first to seventh rounds (see page 62): Start with orange and crochet two rounds. Then work one round each in blue, light green, magenta, orange and blue. When changing colours, work the last slip stitch in the round in the new colour. Increase the loop on the hook, but do not cut the blue yarn.

Secure the ends, then sew on French knots and satin stitches in light green and magenta (see page 38).

Insert the shank button and crochet the back in blue (see page 62).

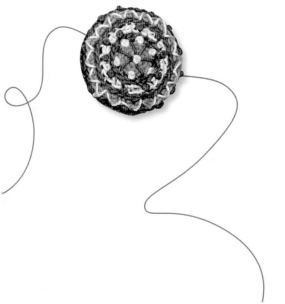

Materials

- very fine crochet yarn in orange, magenta and burgundy
- crochet hook size 10–8 (1.25-1.5mm)
- blank button, approximately 20mm (¾in) diameter
- cotton wadding/batting

How it's done

Crochet the first to fourth rounds in orange (see page 62). Then crochet one round of picots in magenta. Join the magenta yarn at the end of the round with one slip stitch, ★ work three chain stitches, one single crochet (UK double crochet) in the first of the three chain stitches, miss one stitch, and work one single crochet (UK double crochet) into the front loop of the next stitch. Repeat from ★. Finish the round with one slip stitch in the first slip stitch in magenta, then cut the yarn and draw through.

Join burgundy to the back loop of a single crochet (UK double crochet) in orange and work one round as instructed, starting at the beginning of a round, repeating the pattern four times and finishing with one slip stitch in the chain. Work the back the same as the front but without the picots, and all in burgundy. Push the blank button shank through the opening before tightening the loop of thread. Place the front and back together (with the white coat button between) and join with one round of slip stitches. When you are about half way round, stuff the flower with wadding/batting and push into shape.

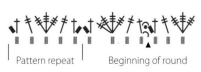

Pattern repeat   Beginning of round

Symbols see page 66

Materials

- metallic crochet yarn in gold for hook size 6 (1.75mm)
- crochet hook size 6 (1.75mm)
- covered black button, 40mm (1½in) diameter

How it's done

Work six chain stitches and join with a slip stitch. Continue working to the pattern. After the third round with three chain stitches, change to the back and work one double crochet (UK treble) and two chain stitches into each chain loop of the third round.

After about half the round, insert the button into the crochet. End the round with one slip stitch and move on to the next round with three chain stitches. Then work one double (UK treble) into each chain loop and finish the round with one slip stitch. Cut the yarn, pull it through and secure.

Symbols

- • = 1 chain stitch
- ⌒ = 1 slip stitch
- T = 1 half double (UK half treble)
- ⋔ = decrease 3 double (UK treble) together
- ⋔⋮ = 3 chain stitches and decrease 2 double (UK treble) together

Crochet diagram

Material

- metallic crochet yarn in gold for hook size 1.75 (US 6)
- crochet hook no. 1.75 (US 6)
- button covered in black, 40mm (1½in) diameter
- 15 transparent beads in anthracite, 2.6mm (1 1/32in) diameter

How it's done

Crochet four chain stitches and work rows one to four as instructed. Repeat rows three and four five more times (= seven petals), then cut the yarn and pull through. Sew the foundation chains and the last row together to make a petal.

Thread fifteen beads (see page 8) and crochet ten bead stitches into the opening in the middle of the bottom (see page 10). In the next round, work one bead stitch into every second stitch, then cut the yarn and pull through.

Join the chains to the tip of a new petal. Work three chain stitches to replace the first double (UK treble), then ★ five chain stitches and one double (UK treble) into the next petal. Repeat ★ five times, work five chain stitches and finish the round with one slip stitch into the top of the three replacement chain stitches. Start the next round with five chain stitches to replace the first double treble (UK triple treble), then work one double treble (UK triple treble) into each double (UK treble) of the previous round.

Finish the round with one slip stitch into the top of the five replacement chain stitches, pull the yarn through and secure.

Crochet diagram

Symbols

- • = 1 chain stitch
- I = 1 single crochet (UK double)
- T = 1 half double (UK half treble)
- † = 1 double crochet (UK treble)
- ‡ = 1 treble (UK double treble)
- ‡ = 1 double treble (UK triple treble)
- ◀ = beginning

Dog, cat, mouse

These animal buttons are adorable with cute faces and loyal, loving eyes. Crochet them in any colour!

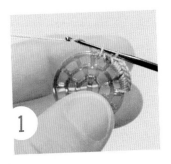
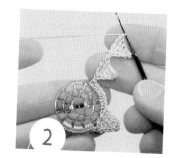
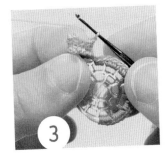
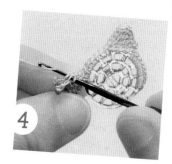

🐾 CROCHETING AROUND A PLASTIC GRID BUTTON

1 The animal faces are crocheted on to plastic grid buttons, which are special transparent plastic buttons for sewing and crocheting. Crochet around the button to join the button top and bottom together:

Join the yarn on an outside opening on the button. Observe the position of the shank in the crochet pattern to make sure that the hook eyes is more or less horizontal on the finished head; the shank should be facing down. Then work single crochet (UK double) into the opening as per the pattern and crochet on the ears.

🐾 CROCHETING EARS
(crochet patterns on page 68)

2 The ears are crocheted on to the head and worked double to make sure they are firm and do not curl up. For the cat, for example, work six chain stitches for the front of the ear, then turn and work single crochet (UK double), half double (UK half treble) etc. into the chain stitch.

Then work six more chain stitches for the back of the ear and continue crocheting to the double treble (UK triple treble).

3 Fold over the back of the ear so that it is below the front part. For the mouse, you can work the loose links of four chains stitches onto the backs of the ears to match. The backs of the dog's ears are not folded over, but instead placed under the front parts of the ears. Like the fronts of the ears, the right sides of the backs point upwards.

4 Insert the hook into the front of the ear from above, take up the back loop (or chain) of the front and back parts of the ear, and work one slip stitch to join them (shown in grey).

🐾 CROCHETING THE FACE
(pattern on page 68)

When the top of the button is finished (see page 68), secure the ends of the black thread used for the nose, and sew on the mouth in backstitch (see page 40). The tip of the dog's and mouse's nose points up, whereas the cat's points down. To make the whiskers, knot together three pieces of black thread about 20cm (7¾in) long in the middle with a double knot. Push the knot into the nose and pull the individual whiskers out using a sewing needle or crochet hook. Use black sewing thread and a sewing needle to secure the whisker knot on the inside.

Then sew on the beads for the eyes. Draw the needle out in the desired spot, thread the white and then the black bead; feed the thread back through the white bead, and push into the crochet. Repeat this process once more. Secure the thread on the inside, and sew on the second eye in the same way. Make sure the thread is well secured.

Materials

- very fine crochet yarn in orange, white (for the mouse), light green (for the cat) and light blue (for the dog)
- very fine crochet yarn in black
- plastic grid button, approximately 22mm (¾in) diameter
- per button: 2 white beads 4mm (²⁄₈in) diameter, 2 black beads 1.8mm (¹⁄₁₆in) diameter
- crochet hook size 10–8 (1.25–1.5mm)
- sewing needle and sharp embroidery needle
- cotton wadding/batting

How it's done

Crochet around the plastic grid buttons, and crochet on the ears (see page 67 and crochet pattern below). Work the faces as shown in the pattern, then start with a loop of black thread (see page 62). At the end of round one, change to the face colour, and start by working the slip stitch in the new colour.

Draw the loop up at the end of the last round (do not cut) and complete the face (see page 67).

Place the face on the bottom of the button and crochet both together around the edge in slip stitches, catching one outside stitch loop on the top and the bottom in your work. On the ears, crochet the top to the loops around the grid head or else to the doubles (UK trebles). A few stitches before the end of the round, stuff the head with wadding/batting and press into shape.

Symbols

- • = 1 chain
- ⌒ = 1 slip stitch
- ▮ = 1 single crochet (UK double)
- T = 1 half double (UK half treble)
- † = 1 double (UK treble)
- ‡ = 1 treble (UK double treble)
- ╪ = 1 double treble (UK triple treble)
- ◄ = beginning

Pattern for the face

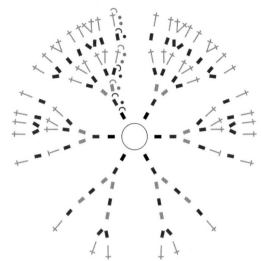

The stitches that meet at the top are decreased together.

Pattern for the cat's ears

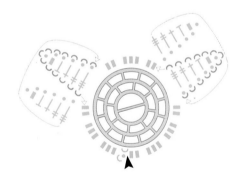

Pattern for the dog's ears

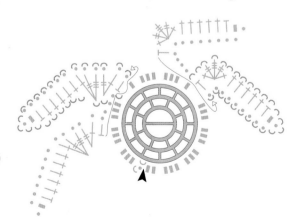

Pattern for the mouse's ears

Twiggy buttons

Collections of driftwood, sticks and small branches are perfect for these novel buttons.

Material

- dry sticks (if you use green wood you run the risk of the buttons splitting as the wood dries – or even starting to rot under the paint)
- white acrylic paint
- brush
- paint markers in various colours
- thin waterproof fineliner in black
- clear varnish
- small screw hooks or rivet pins
- drill (a little smaller than the hook thread or a little thicker than the rivet pin)
- saw
- brush
- course and smooth sandpaper
- skewers or cocktail sticks

How it's done

1 Pull the bark off the sticks. Saw the sticks to the size you want the buttons to be. Smooth the surfaces with the coarse sandpaper, then with the smoother sandpaper. Pre-drill a hole for the hook in the middle, then screw in the hook or drill a small hole through the piece of wood and push in the rivet pin and bend on the bottom to make a shank. Trim any overlapping material.

2 Push the skewer or cocktail stick through the hook so that you can hold the button by it. Prime the button with white acrylic paint and leave to dry.

3 + 4 Draw on dots, lines or patterns with the paint markers. Before adding any overlapping layers, allow the bottom one to dry well first.

Once the paint is dry, draw the contours and tiny dots with the fineliner. Leave the button to dry and then varnish.

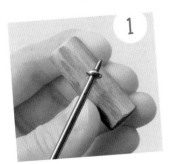

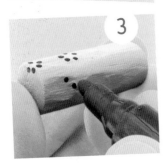

Driftwood buttons

Create a relaxing beach holiday vibe with these charming driftwood buttons.

Materials

- pieces of driftwood
- gold wire, 0.3mm (US 28 guage) diameter, or rivet pin
- drill, 0.4mm (US 26 guage) diameter or a little thicker than the rivet pin
- flat pliers
- wire cutters
- split ring
- if desired, beads, bead caps and pieces of shell with holes etc.

How it's done

1 Gold wire version: Drill a little hole through the wood a little off-centre (at the spot where you want to start winding) and thread the end of the wire through from the top to the bottom.

2 + 3 Wind it tightly around the piece of wood, perhaps including a bead in the middle of the winding on the top, and incorporating the split ring on the back. Push the bead and ring over the end of the wire, keeping the wire as straight as possible. You must not allow any bends or twists in the wire. In order to include the ring the second and third times, carefully pull the wire through the ring without letting it bend.

4 Once you have wound enough wire around the wood, wrap it around the starting point of the ring a few times.

5 Twist the beginning and end of the wire together.

6 Trim the ends of the wire and push them under the windings or ring.

Rivet pin version: drill a hole in the middle of the piece of wood. Push a piece of shell or bead cap onto the pin, then push the rivet pin through the wood and bend the bottom to make a shank. Trim any overlapping material.

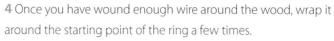

Clay buttons

It's amazing just what you can do with a piece of modelling clay – create animals, flowers, patterns, abstracts and much more.

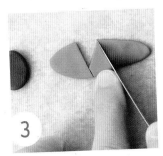

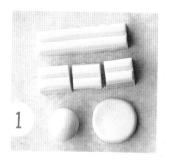

Material

- oven-bake modelling clay in various colours
- split rings or spacers
- glossy varnish for the modelling clay
- acrylic paint
- brush
- knife and round cutters
- skewers or cocktail sticks
- 2 flat wooden sticks approximately 3mm (1/8 in) thick
- stamps, beads etc.
- rolling pin
- baking parchment
- paper towels
- smooth sandpaper

How it's done

1 Cut off a sufficient quantity of equally sized pieces of modelling clay. Kneading makes the clay soft and pliable. Many of these buttons are made by rolling a ball and then flattening it to make a circle or shaping into an oval.

Be sure to use baking parchment as it's easy to pull the modelling clay off of after baking.

2 If you want to attach a shank on the back of the button, push the ring into the clay in the middle of the back. Make a little tie, push it through the ring and smooth it with a knife.

3 To make the bird's head, start by flattening a ball of clay. For the beak, shape a piece about 2mm (1/16 in) thick with your hand and cut out one triangle.

4 + 5 To make the eyes, roll a little line of clay, flatten it slightly and cut two slices out of the middle. Cut the bottom edge off in a straight line. Place the beak and eyes on the head and press down. To make the pupils, roll a thin line of clay and cut off two tiny pieces, then shape into balls and position on the eyes.

6 Two little rolled up pieces of aluminium foil will keep the shank buttons in place when baking them. Shank buttons with a flat top can also be put face down on the baking parchment for baking.

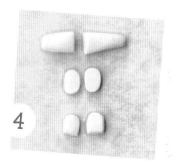

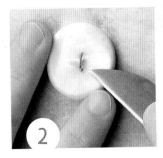

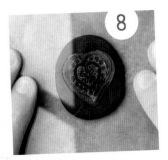

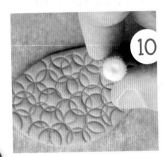

7 To make pieces of equal thickness, place the modelling clay between two wooden planks and roll out with the rolling pin. The clay will then be as thick as the planks.

8 You can use almost any kind of stamp to make a relief-type surface. Either stamp a rolled out surface and then cut out the button, or shape a ball into the desired button and then stamp it.

9 Tiny beads and other buttons can also be used to make a pattern on the surface. Beads are easy to lift off again with a pin or needle as shown. If using shank buttons, attach the shank first and place the button on the two planks (which you have wrapped in aluminium foil) with the shank between the planks.
Then decorate the button.

10 Use the lid of a felt pen, skewers or a knife to create graphic patterns. Work all the way to the edge of the button by pressing in half motifs.

11 + 12 After baking (refer to the manufacturer's instructions), coat the buttons in clear varnish and leave to dry. Then paint the surface in a contrasting colour (acrylic paint) and wipe off with a paper towel so that the paint only remains in the indentations. Apply another layer of clear varnish to the buttons. It is not possible to wipe all of the paint off unvarnished buttons: the whole button is painted, and the colour is much stronger in the indentations. If you like, you can use smooth sandpaper on the raised areas to expose the original colour of the button.

13 For the striped buttons, roll very thin laces out on the baking parchment with flat hands. Place the laces on the rolled-out surface and push down with the rolling pin (running it over the two wooden battens).

Materials

Button A:
- oven-bake modelling clay in white-transparent, yellow, orange and red
- split ring

Button B:
- oven-bake modelling clay in metallic blue and metallic white
- split ring

Button C:
- oven-bake modelling clay in metallic blue and metallic white, alternatively in red and metallic grey
- round cutters, 1.5cm (½in) and 2cm (¾in) diameter
  (see page 74 for other tools and materials)

How it's done

Cut the desired number of pieces out of the various colours for buttons A and B.

Button A: Roll the pieces into balls, then make them into ovals. Attach the ring to the back (see page 74). Cut little pieces off a rolled lace and shape into balls, then place on the button. Press very lightly on the balls so that they sit on the button like tiny nubs.

Button B: Roll the pieces into balls, then place in your cupped hand and shape into a hemisphere. Attach the ring on the back and model the shape a little more if necessary. Top with tiny white balls (see above) and press down flat.

Button C: Roll out one red piece and one blue piece, and place grey stripes on the red piece and white stripes on the blue one. Press down (see page 76).

Cut out the buttons with cutters, making sure the stripes are arranged as desired.

Smooth the edges with your fingers.

Varnish the buttons after baking.

Material

- oven-bake modelling clay in pink, white, black and red
- clear varnish
  (see page 74 for other tools and materials)

How it's done

Start with a large ball of pink for the face. Press the ball down flat. Put on a small ball as the nose and press down flat. To make the ears, squeeze together some little pieces of modelling clay on one side between your index finger and thumb to make a point. Add the ears, bending one if you like, and smooth the base of the ear with a knife.

Roll tiny laces for the eyes (one in white and one very thin one in black), cut off two pieces of the same size and roll into balls (see page 74). Put the balls on the face and press down.

You can decide whether you want the pig to be cross-eyed or have both eyes looking in a particular direction. Add a red line of clay for the mouth, and use the skewer to make two nostril holes pierce all the way through so the head can be sewn on.

Publication details:

First published in Great Britain in 2015 by
Search Press, Wellwood, North Farm Road,
Tunbridge Wells, Kent, TN2 3DR

Original edition © 2013 Christophorus Verlag
GmbH & Co. KG, Freiburg, Germany

World rights reserved by Christophorus Verlag
GmbH & Co. KG Freiburg, Germany

Original German title: *Knöpfe selber machen*

Translation by Burravoe Translation Services

ISBN: 978-1-78221-062-7

Book concept and layout idea: Beate Schmitz
Photos: Uwe Bick
(Photos pages 15, 31, 41, 45, 51 and 53:
Beate Schmitz)
Styling: Beate Schmitz
Drawings and step-by-step photos: Beate Schmitz

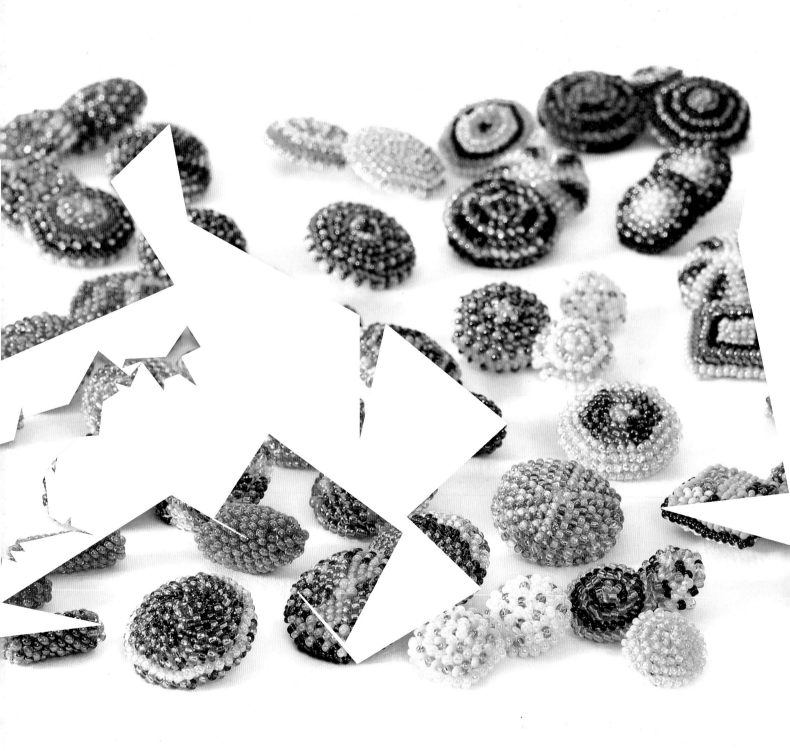